Tried and Tested Talks for Children

Ken Taylor

kevin mayhew

kevin mayhew

First published in Great Britain in 2010 by Kevin Mayhew Ltd
Buxhall, Stowmarket, Suffolk IP14 3BW
Tel: +44 (0) 1449 737978 Fax: +44 (0) 1449 737834
E-mail: info@kevinmayhewltd.com

www.kevinmayhew.com

9 8 7 6 5 4 3 2

ISBN 978 1 84867 267 3
Catalogue No. 1501227

Cover design by Rob Mortonson
© Image copyright Andere
Used under licence from Shutterstock Inc
Edited by Alison Evans
Typeset by Richard Weaver

Printed and bound in Great Britain

Contents

About the author

Ken Taylor is a Methodist minister. Born and educated in Hull, he trained for the ministry in Manchester, and since ordination he has worked in Orrell, St Helens, Liverpool, Leeds (Cross Gates) and Chester-le-Street. He is married with four sons and a daughter. Obliged to retire through ill-health he lived first in Skipton and now in Harrogate.

He is the author of *Sunday by Sunday (Volume 1 and 2): Meditations and resources for all appointed Gospel readings Year A, B and C* and *Cradle of Hope* – all published by Kevin Mayhew.

Introduction

All the following are suitable for addressing children in church. Some are better used in Family Services. Many are suitable for school assemblies; those on pages 75 onwards are 'secular' and especially suitable.

The material for the second to fifth Sundays in Lent could well be used in one family service.

'Harvest Scrabble', 'Sharing an apple', 'The Third World' and 'Tea or coffee' are suitable for use in Harvest festivals and One World Week.

It is recommended that stories and explanations are *not read openly* but simply *told* directly to children.

The 'props' you will need and all suggested actions/answers are printed in *italics.*

Electronic versions of the images are available for download at www.kevinmayhew.com/resources.

ADVENT 1

The day of the cockerel

Hands up if you've seen a church with a spire.

What was on top of the spire? *(A weather vane)*

Yes. It's called a weather vane.
It points north, east, south and west.

What is the one animal normally on top of a weather vane?

Why a cockerel?

Do you know any Bible stories about a cockerel?

Jesus said to Peter, 'Tonight before the cock crows
you will deny me three times.'
It was the night before Jesus was crucified.

And Peter did: three times he said,
'I don't know him and have nothing to do with him.'

And so today is called 'The day of the cockerel.'

I'm very sorry. I should have begun by wishing you a happy new year.

It's Advent Sunday – the beginning of a new year in the Church.

It's called 'The day of the cockerel' because of Peter who was the first disciple. Jesus called him the rock on which the Church is built.

It's called 'The day of the cockerel' because a cockerel crows at the beginning of a new day and this is the beginning of a new year in the Church built on Peter.

And it's called 'The day of the cockerel' because cockcrow is a call for people to wake up – and that's the message from the letter St Paul wrote to the Church in Rome: It's high time to wake up.

Wake up to what God is doing in the world, wake up at the beginning of a new year in the Church, wake up because it's Advent and Christ and Christmas are coming.

ADVENT 2

Coming – ready or not

(Play a simple game of hide and seek with two counting and 'seeking' and ten hiding or one counting and six hiding.)

We're going to play hide and seek.

I need one or two of you to be the seekers and count up to 20 with me while the others hide, and then when we call 'Coming – ready or not' to go and look for them.

(Count from 1 to 20.) Coming – ready or not.

(Once all the children are back in their seats.)

'Coming – ready or not' is the Advent warning to the Church and to us all.

Christmas is coming whether you are ready or not.

Have you bought all the cards you will need? Written them? Hands up if the answer is No. All of you! Grown-ups too!

Christmas is coming whether you are ready or not.

And have you got a tree? And decorations? And have you bought all the presents you want to give? Hands up!

Let this be a warning to you!

Christmas is coming whether you are ready or not.

It's also a reminder and warning to the Church.

Christ is coming whether we are ready or not.

Not only at the end of time, but today.

He may look like a starving African child or a young man sleeping rough or an old lady with Alzheimer's, but it's him. 'Inasmuch as you did it for one of the least of these, you did it for me,' he said.

Christ is coming whether we are ready or not.

ADVENT 3

Mountain views

How many children you can involve depends on how many different levels you can make to represent a mountain.

Abraham will sit on a chair facing the centre aisle.

Second Isaiah will stand halfway up the pulpit steps and Jesus will stand (on a box?) in the pulpit. Position the rest of the children at progressive heights between these.

(Prepare as many name cards – as p.14 – as you will use. You can exclude the names in brackets if need be.)

I'm going to need eight (ten) of you to help me.

Stand in a line facing me, in front of the front pew, tallest on your left, shortest on your right.

Now sit on the floor, with your back against the pew.

(Distribute name cards from left to right.)

When I ask you to stand, hold the name in front of your chest, and face the back of the church.

When you go up a block of flats, the higher you go the more you can see.

It's even more true if you climb a mountain; the higher you climb the further you can see.

Today we are going to make a mountain.

At the moment you can't see the back of the church; but as we go along, the last in the line will be able to see more than the others.

And it's a special mountain, getting ready for the coming of Jesus.

The story of the Jewish people, as we see it in the Old Testament, is like climbing a mountain, the higher they climbed the more of the truth they could see.

(Call the children forward and space them out towards the pulpit.)

ABRAHAM, come and sit on the chair.

ABRAHAM was the first to have any vision at all.

MOSES, stand up.

MOSES was the founder of the nation; led his people to freedom, carved out the Ten Commandments, and could see that the only way people could live together in any harmony was by keeping the Laws.

DAVID, stand on the first step.

DAVID was the best king they ever had. He joined all 12 tribes into one nation, and he built up the largest empire they ever had. Perhaps most importantly he established Jerusalem as their capital city – and it is still the most important city in the world for the world's three major religions – Christianity, Judaism and Islam.

(ELIJAH, stand on the next step.

ELIJAH was the first in the line of the prophets. No other nation has produced such a long line of men who saw more and more of the truth about God, people and the future.)

ISAIAH, stand on the next step.

ISAIAH was one of four prophets, 800 years before Christ, who could see more of the truth about God than anyone before.

(AMOS, stand next to Isaiah.

AMOS was another of those great prophets who lived 800 years before Christ.)

JEREMIAH, stand a little higher.

JEREMIAH, the next in the line of great prophets, understood more clearly how God works in peoples' lives.

SECOND ISAIAH, stand halfway up the pulpit steps.

When most of the people were taken into exile in Babylon, there was a prophet amongst them who was the greatest of the prophets. Sadly, no one knows his name and so the wonderful things he wrote were put at the end of the prophecies of Isaiah from chapter 40 onwards and he is only known as SECOND ISAIAH.

JOHN THE BAPTIST, stand on the step next to the pulpit.

JOHN THE BAPTIST was not a prophet, but Jesus said he was the greatest man who ever lived. He is near the top of the mountain because he saw and recognised who Jesus was.

JESUS, stand on the box in the pulpit.

JESUS is at the top of the mountain. He can see further than anyone else and he alone can see all of the other side of the mountain.

Jesus could / can see more of the truth about God and people and life and death than anyone else.

We need to listen to what he said and learn from him.

ADVENT 4

Mary's secret

Today, the Sunday before Christmas, is Mary's day.

Unfortunately she is often squeezed out by carol services. But she was very special.

Of all the women there have ever been God chose her to care for the baby Jesus, feed him, clothe him, change him, teach him to walk and to talk, guard him, guide him, watch over him and teach him till he became a man.

It was a lot to ask of anyone and she was only a young girl in her mid-teens.

It was a lot to ask of anyone and she was very nervous.

But she had a secret that helped her do what God asked of her.

Years later, when Jesus was a grown man, they were both at a wedding.

Mary was responsible for some of the catering. So when they ran out of wine she turned to Jesus and with a plaintive look told him.

'Oh, mother,' he said, 'what shall I do with you?'

But she knew him better than that and went through to where the servants were working.

'That's my son over there,' she said, pointing him out.

'When he comes through, do whatever he tells you.

'Even if you don't understand,
even if it sounds crazy,
do whatever he tells you –
you can trust him.'

That was her secret.

It was that simple faith
that helped her become the mother of Jesus.

'Even if you don't understand,
even if it sounds crazy,
do whatever he tells you –
you can trust him.'

We would do well to learn from her.

'Even if you don't understand,
even if it sounds crazy,
do whatever he tells you –
you can trust him.'

On Christmas Day

The previous Sunday invite the children to each bring one of their new Christmas presents to show you and the congregation.

Invite the children now to come forward and show you and the people the gifts they have brought.

Suggest that they leave their gifts on the step at the front until the end of the service (!).

At the end of the last carol invite them to come and retrieve their new gifts and say a suitable prayer of thanksgiving before the Benediction.

CHRISTMAS 1

The 12 days of Christmas

Prepare 5 cards to give to children in the conclusion:

12 trees

40 rings

40 cows

140 people
(on reverse: 40 + 36 + 30 + 22 + 12)

184 birds
(on reverse: 12 + 22 + 30 + 36 + 42 + 42)

Do you know that song called 'The 12 days of Christmas'?

It's got something important to teach us if we take careful note of what it actually says.

Can you complete the first line?

On the first day of Christmas my true love sent to me . . .
(a partridge in a pear tree.)

On the second day of Christmas my true love sent to me . . .
(2 turtle doves and a partridge in a pear tree.)

Now that's where we get a bit confused.

If we take what it says, we now have
2 partridges,
2 pear trees,
and 2 turtle doves!

On the third day of Christmas my true love sent to me . . .
(3 French hens, 2 turtle doves and a partridge in a pear tree.)

And now that makes
3 partridges,
3 pear trees,
4 turtle doves,
as well as 3 French hens!

On the fourth day of Christmas my true love sent to me . . .
(4 calling birds, 3 French hens, 2 turtle doves and a partridge in a pear tree.)

On the fifth day of Christmas my true love sent to me . . .
(5 golden rings, 4 calling birds, 3 French hens, 2 turtle doves and a partridge in a pear tree.)

On the sixth day of Christmas my true love sent to me . . .
(6 geese a-laying, 5 golden rings, 4 calling birds, 3 French hens, 2 turtle doves and a partridge in a pear tree.)

That's halfway through
and if we take it literally we have now received
6 geese
10 gold rings
12 calling birds
12 French hens
10 turtle doves
6 partridges
and 6 pear trees.

We could go on like this. It works out at:
12 days of partridge and pear tree
2 turtle doves for 11 days
3 French hens for 10 days

4 calling birds for 9 days
5 golden rings for 8 days
6 geese for 7 days
7 swans for 6 days
8 maids and 8 cows for 5 days
9 lords for 4 days
10 ladies for 3 days
11 pipers for 2 days
and on the last day 12 drummers.

That adds up to *(ask a child to hold each card displaying a total)*:
12 trees
40 Rings
40 Cows
40 + 36 + 30 + 22 + 12 = 140 people
12 + 22 + 30 + 36 + 42 + 42 = 184 birds

WOW!

I told you the song had some important things to teach us.

Love is very generous, very reliable and entirely consistent.

And because God is love, love supreme, what he gives is new every morning, and the blessings and benefits increase as time goes by.

Trust him and thank him for his generous love.

Strange gifts

A couple of years ago I received a rather amusing Christmas card:

The three magi came into the house where the holy family were and the first one said, 'We have brought gifts of gold, frankincense, and something really useful.'

When I looked at the drawing, I saw that the 'something really useful' was a large pack of disposable nappies!

It was a good point because gold, frankincense, and myrrh were of no use to Jesus at all.

He had no use for gold – and he never had two shekels to rub together.

Incense was used in special religious rituals but he came to teach a religion much more than special ceremonies and buildings, a religion of love as wide as life and when the women came with myrrh to his tomb on Easter morning he was already up and gone.

Ah yes.

Someone realised that they are symbolic gifts but they are not symbols of Jesus – as king, priest, and saviour.

If you give someone a symbolic gift it's not a symbol of them but of you.

My wife / husband / friend gave me this ring
to remind me of them, not to remind me of me.

The gold, frankincense, and myrrh were not symbols of Jesus but of **them, the Magi.**

They came from a world where people thought money or gold could buy anything, and religion was about special ceremonies and buildings, and where everything grew old and eventually died.

They brought and gave this baby Jesus the best that they knew . . . but he did not need their gifts . . . and he brought far greater gifts.

Give him the best that you know . . .

and he gives you far greater gifts:
love that is beyond price,
love as wide as life itself
and eternal life in love that never dies.

COVENANT SUNDAY

The yoke of Christ

For Methodist people the first Sunday of a new year is known as Covenant Sunday when, as John Wesley urged, they renew their Covenant with God.

All Christian teachers will find this idea useful.

(You will need scarves for the children to use in a three-legged race.)

I was hoping we could have a three-legged race today but there isn't really room for a race.

However, we can have a three-legged procession, so will you get in pairs and get ready with one of these scarves?

(Have some adult volunteers on hand to help the children tie their legs together.)

The procession will go up the side aisle and back down the centre. Off you go!

(When they are back and seated again:)

How did you manage?

Did you find you had to walk in step?

And did you have to hold on to each other to keep from falling over?

That's important. It might help us to understand something the grown-ups will all say in a special new year's service:

We take upon ourselves with joy the yoke of obedience.

When Jesus talked about his yoke he was thinking of two oxen yoked together to pull a plough, having to walk side by side and sharing the weight between them.

Taking his yoke upon ourselves is a bit like a three-legged race.

It means trying to keep in step with him, matching your pace to his.

You can't see him or feel his arm around you but he is there, travelling alongside you, and sharing the load.

EPIPHANY 2

Christingle

(You will need the resources to make a Christingle: a large orange or grapefruit, five cocktail sticks, five jelly babies or dolly mixtures, and a candle. If there are not too many children give them each a small bag containing a tangerine and the rest of the kit for them to take home to make their own.)

On this special Sunday we're going to make a Christingle.

To begin with

What shape is the world? *(Round)*

Well, it's not exactly round – it's a bit flat at the top and bottom. Does anyone know the posh and more accurate word for the shape of the world? *(An oblate spheroid)*

Yes, that's right, an oblate spheroid. It's a bit like the shape of an orange/grapefruit. *(Show yours)*

Do you know the symbol of the Olympic Games, which all the world joins in with? *(Five rings)*

Why are there five? *(There are five continents.)*

Do you know which are the five continents? *(Europe, America, Africa, Asia, and Australasia.)*

Now we can put them and their people into our 'world'.

(Place five sticks with sweets attached in the orange.)

The important message today is that Christ is the Light of the world, the whole world.

(Set the candle in place.)

That's a Christingle.

It says that Christ is the Light of the world and he brings new light to all the peoples of the world.

(Light the candle and lead a suitable prayer.)

We have put Christingle kits together. Please take one home, make your own Christingle, and put it lit at the centre of your dinner table.

I H S

(If you don't have an I H S pulpit fall prepare a card with this logo and cards for each of the words in heavy type.)

You see this cloth hanging down from the pulpit?

Do you know what it's called?

That's right, it's a pulpit fall.

Sometimes a pulpit fall has just three letters like this:

I H S

Any idea what the letters stand for?

They are very special letters in three languages – Greek and Latin and English.

In Greek it's the first three letters of Jesus' name:

I H S Y S

J E S U S

In Latin it stands for

Iesu Hominorum Salvator

which means 'Jesus, Saviour of men [all people]'.

And in English it stands for

In His Service or **In His Steps**

The message is plain:

Jesus is the Saviour of all people.

To serve him you need to follow in his steps,

which means following his example

and trying to do what he says.

We are reminded of that every time we see these letters:

I H S

A bucketful of seawater

When I was a child we used to go for a seaside holiday at Scarborough

and after I'd spent a day on the beach my mother would give me a bucket and send me to get a bucketful of seawater.

I filled the bucket to its brim and carried it back very, very carefully, trying not to spill a drop.

When I got back my mother would sit me on the wall and pour the water over my feet to wash off the sand before she put my sandals back on to walk to where we were staying.

You could have learned quite a lot about the sea from that bucketful.

It tasted like sea. If you had the proper instruments and know-how you could show that it had the same density and specific gravity as the sea.

But there is so much about the sea you could not have learned from that bucketful.

A bucketful gives you no idea of its great depths, its different currents, the many varieties of life it sustains, or its awesome power.

During his earthly life Jesus was like a bucketful of God.

In Jesus of Nazareth you can see as much of the nature and essence of God as your mind can hold – and we can learn so much from him.

But you cannot see in Jesus the great depths of God, all the different currents within him, the many varieties of life he sustains, or his awesome power.

You have to learn from Jesus as much of the truth about God as you can grasp.

But always remember that there is so much more to his nature and his love than you can grasp.

LENT 1

A tug-of-war

(Fasten a long rope or clothes line round your waist so there is enough for 3 or 4 children to pull on each side. Hold the rope on each side of you so they do not pull you over or bruise your waist!)

We're going to have a tug-of-war with me in the middle, so I want six volunteers who won't pull too hard!

You know how sometimes you have to make a very hard decision or choice?

OK, pull! *(Sway from side to side as they pull.)*

I find it hard to decide which way to go – it's a bit like being in the middle of a tug-of-war.

Stop pulling!

It was like that for Jesus in the wilderness as he got ready for his ministry.

This is what we remember in the 40 days of Lent as we prepare for Easter.

Start pulling again. *(Sway from side to side.)*

Jesus got very hungry with fasting and had to decide whether to make bread for himself.

But he had decided not to eat in the wilderness, so would that be giving in to his own needs and breaking his promise to himself?

He wanted to set up a new kingdom and wondered if he should call together an army to fight, but would that be forcing people to do what he wanted?

He could see the tops of the Temple in the distance and wondered if he should jump off and astound people with his power, but decided that would not be the loving way to persuade people to trust him.

When we have to make a hard decision and feel we are being pulled two ways we have to do what he did:

1. Keep our promises
2. Not try to force people to do what we want
3. Decide to do the loving thing.

And when we have decided which way to pull,
the other side will pull even harder
and we have to be very strong to stick to our decisions.

LENT 2

The treasured Cross

(You need two separate cards with the drawings below. Show the map of treasure island.)

Do you know what this is a map of? *(Treasure island)*

How do you where the treasure is buried? *(By the cross)*

Yes, **X** marks the spot. The cross is a sign of treasure.

Over the next few weeks, as we get ready for Good Friday and Easter, we're going to look at different places where we see a cross and think about what that reminds us of, why the Cross of Jesus is treasured by Christians and, like this one *(indicate it)*, central in our church.

Tell me of places where you can see a cross. I'm making notes for coming weeks.

Who said on an ambulance or Red Cross station?

(Show the Red Cross sign.)

This cross is a sign of help if you are injured or need help.

Some people treasure the Cross of Jesus because it is a reminder of the healing and help that he gives.

LENT 3

The treasure of sins forgiven

(Have all posters displayed and added to week by week.)

We're looking at different places where we see a cross to see why the Cross of Jesus is treasured.

Last week we saw that people treasure the Cross of Jesus because of the healing and help that he gives.

Somebody whose maths book I ought not to have seen, said

2 + 2 = 5 X

A cross is a reminder that we all get things wrong and make mistakes – sometimes quite serious ones.

Perhaps the most important thing about the Cross of Jesus is that he earned forgiveness for us and crossed out the guilt of our sins.

It's hard to understand how but by his death on the cross we are forgiven any and all of the wrong we have done.

People treasure the Cross of Jesus because it is a reminder of the healing and help that he gives, and a sign that by his death we are forgiven.

LENT 4

Added treasure

So far this Lent we have learned that the Cross is a reminder of the healing and help that Jesus gives, and a sign that by his death we are forgiven.

Last week's sum that was wrong also had the cross sign we see most often:

2 + 2 = 4

The + sign is very important because it's about what is *added.*

Many people treasure the Cross because Jesus adds joy and hope and peace to their lives because they are forgiven.

And a cross is the centre of a compass.

The compass points north, east, south and west which reminds us that Jesus is for everybody.

So some people treasure the Cross of Jesus because he offers forgiveness, healing and help, joy and hope and peace to anyone and everyone.

LENT 5

At a crossroads

We have been looking at different places we might see a cross.

One of the most obvious is on a journey when you come to a crossroads – and you have to decide which way to go.

You can also make a cross by writing a capital 'I' and then crossing it out.

If you decide to follow Jesus and choose his way and not your own, it will mean putting yourself last – which is like crossing out your own desires and wants.

At the crossroads of this Lent,
if you do choose to go the way of Jesus
you will find his Cross represents a real treasure

because he will give you forgiveness, help and healing, and new hope and real peace and lasting joy.

Litany for Palm Sunday

(This can be used following the 'Palm Crosses' address.)

Hosanna!
Hosanna in the highest!
Blessed is he who comes in the name of the Lord:

Lord Jesus Christ,
We raise these palms to greet your coming,
these crosses to adore your love.

Shepherd King of Peace,
we greet your coming with joy.

Eternal King of kings,
may your **kingdom** come.

Royal King of Love,
come and rule in our lives.

We believe
in the sign of your Cross you will conquer.

Gladly we affirm
Jesus Christ is Lord.

Hosanna!
Blessed is he who comes in the name of the Lord.

LENT 6

Palm Crosses

A couple of years ago I saw two lads holding their Palm Crosses like daggers and pretending to have a sword fight! Don't do that!

You're supposed to hold it like this. *(Demonstrate how.)*

Mind you, I can see it can look like a dagger – and that reminds me of Judas.

His second name was Iscariot – and that could be something to do with a dagger.
It might mean 'the man from Kerioth', a southern village.
Or Iscariot might come from Sicarii – which means dagger-bearers, a band of nationalist assassins.

In any case, dagger-bearer suits him because he was quite sure that the only way for Jesus to establish the Kingdom was by violence and fighting.

In fact, when he betrayed Jesus in Gethsemane he was sure that would happen: 'Now, Lord, now. You are surrounded – call for the angels!'

Holding a Palm Cross like a dagger is the way of Judas; the other way is the way of Jesus.

Choose the way of Jesus.

Responsive Litany of Holy Week

(Use this at the end of Palm Sunday morning so the children know what's coming, and at the beginning of Easter worship.)

This is (has been) the most important week in the history of the world. We shall share this Litany together.

On Sunday (Last Sunday)
the Shepherd King came riding.

On Monday
he cleared the Temple Court.

On Tuesday
he was teaching his disciples.

On Wednesday
he was anointed with oil that Mary brought.

On Thursday
he had supper with his friends and spelt out love
in broken bread and wine.
That night he was betrayed, arrested, tried,
abused and scorned,
and still showed love divine.

On Friday morning
he was crucified,
forgiving those who nailed him to the tree;
all-loving till the moment that he died;
undying love to set the whole world free.

He died as he had lived,
the perfect way of love,
still faithful to the Father's will
victorious love to prove.

On Sunday (today)
it is Easter.

and he is alive again and back with his friends.

Come and celebrate.

Easter eggs

(It would be helpful if you had two rubber or terracotta decoy eggs – otherwise use Cadbury's crème eggs. If it's not too expensive give each child a crème egg after the service or organise an egg-hunt in the church grounds or schoolroom.)

Do you know why we have Easter eggs?

Yes/Well . . .

Jesus died and was buried on Friday afternoon and a large stone was rolled across the entrance to the tomb.

Jewish Law forbade anybody to go on the Sabbath day, but very early on the Sunday morning two or three of his closest women friends came to complete the burial rites which there was not time for before the Sabbath started at dusk on Friday.

On the way they suddenly remembered the large stone and wondered how they would move it but when they got near, surprise! It had already been rolled away!

As you know, today we are celebrating that Jesus rose from death and is alive for ever and the stone being rolled away became a popular sign of it.

Children began to play a game about it.

(Select two children as volunteers.)

You two come out to the front and roll this egg backwards and forwards between you.

(As the children roll the egg.)

An egg seemed the nearest they could get to a round stone
that would roll and it was also a source of new life.

Then because they wanted it to roll somebody tried to roll it
down a hill and started the idea of egg-races.

But eggs break very easily so they tried hard-boiled eggs.

And then because it's so very special
somebody thought of decorating hard-boiled eggs.

And then not so very long ago some sweet manufacturer
had the bright idea of making Easter eggs of chocolate.
What a good idea!

But don't forget:
All this is because the stone was rolled away
and the tomb was empty
and Jesus is alive for evermore.

The next two addresses are concerned with Holy Communion and may be of most use in Family Communion services.

EASTER 2

Sacramentum

(Have enough 20p or 50p pieces to spread along the communion rail for each child to take one.)

When this country was ruled by Queen Victoria we had a large empire.

That meant we needed a very large army with soldiers in many countries.

And that meant we needed a lot of men to 'sign on' in the army.

The big problem was that most people couldn't read or write so 'signing on' in the army was very difficult.

As you would expect they found a solution.

The recruiting sergeant set up a table in a market place
and put one day's pay on the front of the table.
It was known as 'the Queen's shilling'.

Anyone who gave his name and picked up the money was enlisted in the army.

Picking up 'the Queen's shilling' was a vow of allegiance:
Yes, I will serve my Queen and country and will fight to preserve the Empire, and I will give my life if need be.

Roman centurions used to do the same.

Every time a town or city was conquered they had to recruit more men to be trained in the Roman army.

They put a day's pay on a table in the market place and invited men to 'join up'.

Picking up the coin was regarded as a vow of allegiance: Yes, I will serve the Emperor and Empire, and I will fight and give my life if need be for the Roman Empire.

That coin and that vow was called a sacramentum!

The sacrament of Holy Communion is just the same which is why it's called a sacrament – it's a vow of allegiance.

Yes, I will serve Jesus the King and give myself to serve his kingdom.

When we are given and accept a piece of bread *(or wafer)* it's a sacramentum – a vow of allegiance to serve Jesus and his kingdom.

I have put a line of 20p (50p) pieces on the Communion rail – it's not a day's pay but only a symbol!

So come and stand at the rail.

And say with me, 'I will serve King Jesus and his kingdom.'

Together: **I will serve King Jesus and his kingdom.**

And now pick up the coin.

(Teachers may suggest to what the money is given.)

EASTER 3

Holy Communion joins

(This clearly needs adapting for churches who use wafers but the meaning is still vital.)

Do you know who prepares the bread and wine for Holy Communion?

He or she is called the Communion steward.

They cut a slice of bread into small pieces for us to share.

If all the pieces were joined together they would make one slice

and in the same way we who share the pieces are joined together and become one family or fellowship.

Sometimes we use a service which has the words:

Although we are many, we are one body,
because we all share in one bread.

But it's not only about us.

In a very real and important way we are joined in one

with all the people at . . . parish church

with all the people at . . . Catholic church

and all the people who are sharing bread together in this town/village.

It's even more wonderful than that:

we share broken bread as Jesus told us to do

and he joins us into one family with all his people in the world – the whole world.

That's wonderful and amazing!

EASTER 4

An Eastern shepherd

(You will need a private list of the Christian names of all the children present to refer to as you walk.)

I'm going to walk round the church.

When I call your name please follow me.

(As you walk down a side aisle call names separately without turning round or looking back until all the children are following. Walk down the centre aisle to the front and address the children as they stand there.)

It was just like that for a shepherd and his sheep when Jesus lived in Palestine.

Often at night three or four shepherds would bring their sheep inside a walled field for the night – to keep them safe from any thieves or wild animals that were prowling around.

There was no gate but one of the shepherds spent the night in the gap in the wall so that no animal could get in or out. He was himself the gate to the sheepfold.

And the sheep all mingled together.

In the morning a shepherd would set off, calling as he went, without turning round, and the sheep would follow – just like when I called and you followed me.

Read John 3:3b–4; 7, 9, 14 (or A. Dale's *New World*, p.325)

When he calls, you follow.

EASTER 5

The bridge

by Jane Jolly[1]

David lived in a large city. Everything in this city was grey. There was no colour anywhere except when a new baby was born.

When he was a baby David was a healthy colour and full of life. Then as he grew into a child his life began to be tainted by the lives of those around him.

The healthy colour left him. He looked just as grey as those around him. He learned to fight and swear from those he lived with. He struggled through school never ever fulfilling his potential.

As he grew up he glimpsed how he wanted his life to be but events would conspire to prevent him from ever moving in that direction.

Everything around him was grey and dismal. He moved from one unsatisfactory job to another, never finding anything which would give his life meaning.

One day he decided he would try to leave the city but not having much money, he didn't think he would get very far.

He had no idea which roads led away from the city. Each day he would try a new road, only to find that it led right back to where he had started.

1. Used with permission. Jane Jolly is a retired school teacher, now working as a full-time pastoral assistant in the Skipton and Grassington Methodist Circuit.

Then one day he came across some people who looked totally different from the people he had grown up with. They wore clothes of brilliant colours. They looked happy. They didn't swear; they didn't push or shove. They told him of a life beyond the city where people were happy and had found a truly satisfying way to live.

'How do I get there?' he asked.

'You just have to cross the bridge at the end of this street.'

'What bridge?'

'It's a bridge that has been there as long as we can remember,' they said. 'People say that long ago this place was joined to the land on the other side of the bridge. People were happy then. Life was colourful and bright.

Then the grimy, grey seas flooded around the city, cutting it off from the land beyond.

No one knew what to do. They tried to build ships that would take them across the sea but these always sank just a short way out from the shore.

Then one day a man appeared who started to build a bridge across to the other side.

He said his father had sent him and this was to be his life's work.

Building the bridge was hard and painful. No one could help him. Whenever anyone tried, that part of the bridge would just crumble away into the sea. The day the bridge was completed, he died.

It was very strange.

From that day onwards it has been possible to leave this grey and horrible life behind. And when you cross over you can meet the man who built the bridge. How, no one is quite sure.'

'But if this bridge has been here for so long, why haven't more people crossed it?' David asked.

'Perhaps because no one has ever told them about it,' they replied.

'Do I have to pay someone to get onto the bridge?' he asked.

'No, there is no charge,' they replied. 'You just have to believe that this bridge will take you to a better life. Then you keep going. Don't turn round; and don't look back.'

EASTER 6

To infinity and beyond!

Hands up if you have heard of Buzz Lightyear.

Can anyone tell me his cry as he takes off?

(To infinity and beyond!)

That's right – whatever it means!

I can't understand it
but it's a very good slogan for last Thursday

and I can't really understand that either,

but I *can* tell you what it means.

Last Thursday was Ascension Day
– it's the day we celebrate
that after his death and resurrection
and the time that his friends saw the risen Christ,
Jesus went back to heaven.

Nobody can really understand that
but we *can* know what it means:

There's a church in Italy called the Church of the Ascension
and on the ceiling is painted a cloud
with two feet sticking out of the bottom!

It wasn't really like that.

We're talking about things we can't see or hear or touch,
about things beyond human experience,
about new dimensions.

When Jesus said he was going to the Father
he meant he was going from one time and one place
to every place all the time.

I don't really understand how
but I know it means that he is always with me
and I am never alone.

The last time his friends saw him
his hands were raised in blessing
and that's the way it always is –
Christ is blessing us – more than we realise.

Ascension Day also celebrates that Jesus is King of all creation and King of all kings and rulers.

Ascension Day reminds us that Jesus our King is always with us and always blessing us.

Happy birthday, Church family

(This depends entirely on candles that relight themselves after being blown out. Set a sufficient number of such lit candles on a suitable, iced cake.)

Did you know that today is called Pentecost and is the birthday of the whole worldwide Church?

And so, we have got to have a birthday cake.

(Invite a group of the youngest children
to stand around the cake and sing.)

Happy birthday to you,
happy birthday to you,
happy birthday, Church family,
happy birthday to you.

Ask them to blow out the candles . . . and again . . . and again.

That's the truth about the Church:
its light can never be put out.

PENTECOST

What is a church?

(You will need:
apron
brick
hymn book
insurance policy
gym kit
antique item
bag of money
old school tie
family photo of adults and children
opened umbrella
school satchel
cross.)

(Hold up brick and apron.)

What have these two things in common?

(Without explaining, get two children to the front to hold up the brick and apron and a third to hold a family photo.)

Any ideas what these three things have in common?

(Again, without explaining, get all 12 items held by a line of children at the front.)

What have all these things in common?

They are all things that some people think a church is!

And most of them are wrong!

We're going to build up a picture of a church, and that means we have to get rid of those things that do not fit.

(As you dispose of the next items the children return to their places until only five remain.)

The Church is made of people, and although they meet in a building the Church is not a building.
People – not bricks and mortar – are the Church.
So we can get rid of the *brick*.

Some people think belonging to the Church is a kind of insurance to make sure they go to heaven when they die, but they will anyway
and we can get rid of the idea of an *insurance policy*.

Others think that all the Church cares about is getting money. That's just rubbish and we can get rid of the *bag of money*.

The Church is not an exclusive club,
so goodbye to the *old school tie*.

Nor is it a kind of museum preserving old-fashioned things that are out-of-date.
We can get rid of the *old antique*.

The Church is not a sort of gymnasium to keep us spiritually fit.

So we don't need a *gym kit*.

And, although some people expect it, going to church does not keep you safe from the storms of life.
So you can close the *umbrella* and give it back to me.

Now, what have we got left?

(As you move through the remaining five items, position the children accordingly.)

The *family photo* is important and right.
The Church is made of people – adults and children.
So you sit in the middle.

And we are all trying to learn more about Jesus and his way so the *school satchel* belongs in our picture.
You stand on one side of the family.

We are learning that we should serve other people:
so put on the *apron* and stand on the other side.

The first activity of the Church is worship, so behind and above the family we must hold the *hymn book*.

And over and above everything we must hold the *Cross* of Jesus who died to make all people into one family.

And that's the Church:

a family of worship and service learning from Jesus.

Catseyes

Have you ever sat in the front of a car at night and seen a line of lights down the middle of the road?

And what are they called? *(Catseyes)*

They were invented by a very clever man called Percy Shaw from Halifax. By this amazing invention he has prevented hundreds of accidents and saved the lives of scores of people.

Did you know they have eyelids?

Well, soon after the first ones were installed it rained and the traffic made the catseyes very muddy and they would not reflect any light.

So they were adapted with 'eyelids' so that when a car or lorry ran over them they were briefly shut and the rubber 'eyelids' cleaned the mud off.

When I was a child I used to stand on them when I was crossing the road and that made the water squirt out!
My mother was not pleased.

I once asked some children how they work. I was told there is a tunnel running down the middle of the road, manned by squads of elves!

A look-out elf shouts, 'There's a car coming!'
and another elf runs along the tunnel, flicking on the lights until he comes to the next checkpoint when another elf takes over. Meanwhile, another elf is coming along switching off the lights.

No, of course I don't believe in elves either.

Clearly it's about reflection.

Mirrors in the catseyes catch and reflect the light from an approaching car's headlights.

The catseyes have no wires, batteries or light within themselves.

It's a bit like when Jesus told his followers, 'You are light for all the world.'

It's all about reflection.

We have no light within ourselves but if we can reflect from
Jesus the light of love and care
we shall help people on their life's journey.

How many books?

(This address will differ depending on whether your Bible translation includes the Apocrypha.)

How many books am I holding up? *(One)*

Think more carefully – Old and New Testaments – now how many? *(Two/three)*

The latest translations include some books inserted between the Old and New Testaments –
dating from 200 BC to 100 AD – and together they are called The Apocrypha.

But I am not holding just two *(or three)* books.

The Bible is like a whole library of books.

Any ideas how many books in the Old Testament? *(There are 39.)*

And what about the New Testament? *(There are 27.)*

The Apocrypha has 15 books.

That means I am holding not one
but a library of 66/81 books altogether.

And they are not all the same, they can be roughly categorised as:

	OT	*NT*	*Apocrypha*
Law	5		
History	10		6
Prophecy	15		
Hymns	1		
Wisdom	6		2
Stories	1		3
Diaries		1	
Visions	1	1	3
Letters		21	1
Gospels		4	

Most of them are very important

but the most important of all are the four Gospels.

Matthew, Mark, Luke and John do not always agree in very small details

but the Gospels were written to give us a clear picture of Jesus, his teaching, and what he has achieved for us.

Try reading a Gospel story about Jesus every day

and get for yourself as clear a picture of him, his teaching, and his love as you can.

Sticklebacks

(You need two cardboard fishes, painted on each side, and fastened on separate sticks so you can illustrate the action.)

Early one morning Sammy Stickleback woke up and thought he would go for a swim.

So he set off from his nest...

Did you know that sticklebacks have nests?

Sammy was swimming along quite happily for a while

and then quite suddenly he came face to face with Cyril Stickleback, and Cyril was looking very fierce.

Sammy quickly turned round and swam back the way he had come as fast as he could – hotly pursued by Cyril.

Fairly soon he began to slow down but Cyril did not catch him because he was swimming slower as well.

They got slower and slower – until Sammy suddenly turned round to face Cyril – who also turned round and swam away as fast as he could – hotly pursued by Sammy.

Gradually they both got slower and slower – until quite suddenly Cyril turned round to face Sammy – and Sammy turned round and swam away as quickly as he could.

Gradually they started to swim slower and slower again – until... guess what! Sammy suddenly turned round and faced Cyril who also turned tail and swam away.

They could well have been doing that all day long – backwards and forwards, going fast, and then slower and slower.

Sticklebacks are like that, and seem to spend a lot of the time chasing each other backwards and forwards, getting slower and slower until they suddenly turn and swim the other way.

And it's not as crazy as it sounds.

When they are near to their own nest they are very confident and brave. But the further they go from home the less confident they feel – and need to get back as soon as they can.

Christians can be like that about their church. It can be very frightening in the world and we have to keep coming back to church to renew our confidence.

As you get older don't ever think you can manage without your friends in the church. Keep coming, for this is where you will find the confidence to keep following Jesus.

A vital word-square

(You need a large card or flipchart with the word-square printed in large letters and the PATERNOSTER cross on the reverse side or next sheet.)

Mount Vesuvius erupted in 70 AD and totally destroyed the famous ancient city of Pompeii.

Amongst the ruins was found the body of a man wearing a mysterious armband with the words:

S	A	T	O	R
A	R	E	P	O
T	E	N	E	T
O	P	E	R	A
R	O	T	A	S

Starting at the top left and reading across it says

SATOR AREPO TENET OPERA ROTAS

Starting at the same square and reading each column down from left to right it says the same!

SATOR AREPO TENET OPERA ROTAS

Now start at the bottom right-hand corner and read all the lines from right to left and the columns upwards from right to left.

and it says the same twice more!

That's four times, in every direction, up, down and sideways, north, south, east and west.

SATOR AREPO TENET OPERA ROTAS

It must be very important but what does it mean?

It seems like Latin but even people who are good at Latin can't understand it.

Then a man who was clever at anagrams and good at Latin had an idea (he would have done well on *Countdown*!)

4 As, 4 Ts, 4 Os, 4 Rs, 4 Es, 2 Ss, 2 Ps, and 1 N

That almost makes PATERNOSTER twice

PATERNOSTER is the Latin for 'Our Father'.

But we are still 1 N short . . .

Unless we write it in a Cross:

P
A
T
E
R
P A T E R N O S T E R
O
S
T
E
R

And he'd cracked it!

Wherever you go, north, south, east, or west,
pray as Jesus taught us . . . Our Father . . .

God, who is our Father in heaven, loves you and cares for you.

You can trust him.

Sharing the peace

(Involve different children until you have 4 or 6 at the front.)

Do you know what a 'high five' is?

Will you two come and give me a 'high five' please?

What does it mean? *(Congratulations – like scoring a goal.)*

What do you do if I say 'Give me five'?

Who started that? *(West Indians)*

So – it's a West Indian handshake.

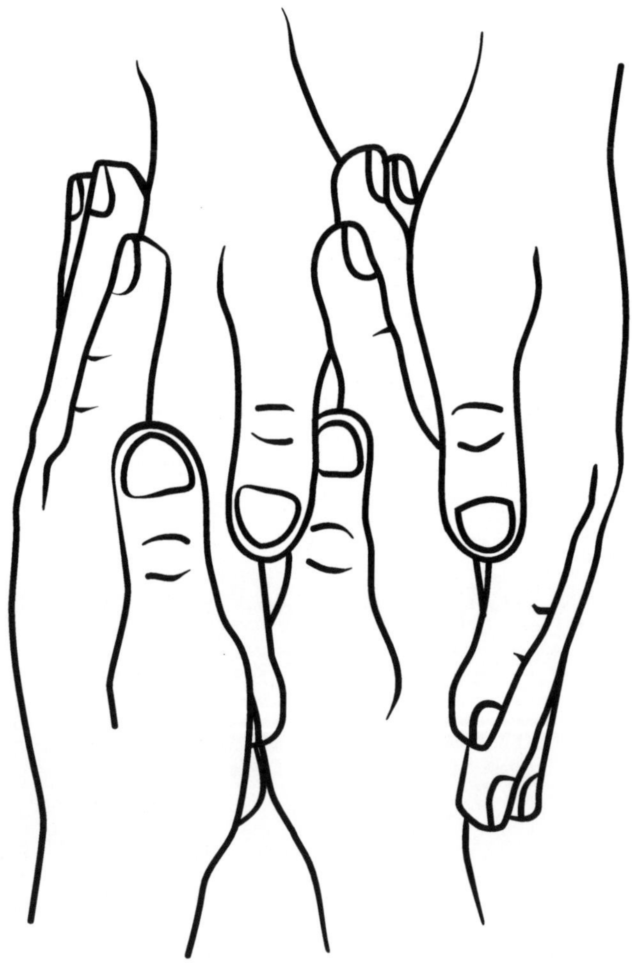

Do you know a boxer's handshake?

(Both fists clenched and 'punching' each other's.)

Do you know a Roman soldier's handshake?

(Grasp each other's forearm with right hand.)

Seems a bit tough – but it was to make sure that the other wasn't carrying a knife hidden up their sleeve!

Do you know a businessman's handshake?

(Firm grasp of right hands.)

Do you know a farmer's handshake?

(Spit on right hand before shaking hands.)

Do you know a Christian's handshake?
No, it's not just like a businessman's. It's very special.

Will one of you come and demonstrate the handshake with me?
Put your right palm against mine, without holding on.
And now we put our left hands at the sides –
almost like a hand sandwich!

I say 'Peace be with you'; you reply 'And also with you.'

There's no holding on or grasping, just touching.
It's called the kiss of peace.

Now go down the aisles and give the peace to the person at the end of each row and they will pass 'the Peace' greeting along the row.

Salt

If someone calls at your house your mum will probably say 'Would you like a cup of tea or coffee . . . and would you like a biscuit?'

You will not find that kind of hospitality everywhere in the world.

There are some countries, especially in the Middle East, where people are very cautious about whom they will eat and drink with until they know them really well and trust them.

Do you know how, in the past, two Red Indians would cut their hands and then put the two cuts together so that their blood mingled?

And then they said, 'We are now blood brothers' – and that meant they had vowed to do anything for each other – even to give their life for each other if need be.

Although I wouldn't recommend literally becoming blood brothers, there are some countries where people think that eating and drinking with other people is like becoming 'blood brothers'.

It was like that in Palestine when Jesus was growing up and living there.

People who 'broke bread' together thought they were like 'blood brothers'.

Salt was very important in cooking and because there is salt in bread, sharing bread together was called 'the fellowship of salt'.

Do you remember how that great crowd of 5000 people wanted Jesus to lead them as an army and drive out the Romans?

He had no intention at all of fighting but he wanted them to know he pledged himself like a 'blood brother' to them and wanted them to pledge themselves to each other.

So in his miracle for them he took five small loaves and sharing them was a pledge of loyalty to each other in the 'fellowship of salt'.

Eleven of the disciples could not forgive Judas for betraying Jesus but what made it even worse for them was that at the Last Supper it was *'after he had received the bread'* that Judas went out to betray Jesus.

It's still the same in Holy Communion. Sharing the bread is a fellowship of salt and we pledge ourselves to do anything for him and for each other.

Jesus

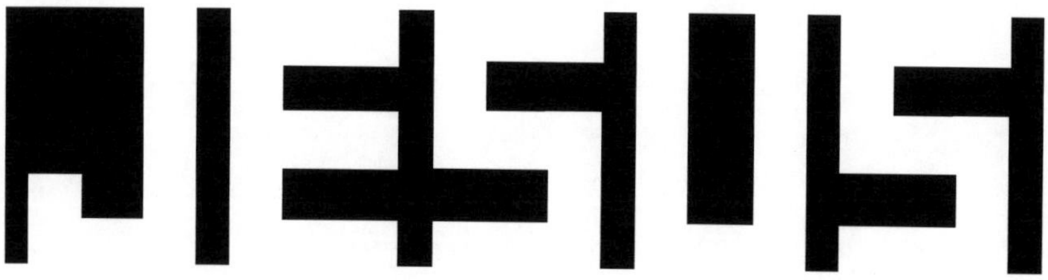

Can you see what this says?

You have to look deeper into the background.

Now can you see what it says?

(Show first letter)

Can you see what letter this is?

And this one?

What about this one?

How about this one? 

And another . . . 

Now can you see what this says? *(Turn 'JESUS' from side to side.)*

Seeing Jesus is sometimes like that. You think you can see him quite clearly and then a moment later you can't.

I keep his name on top of a bookshelf and I can always see what it says.

That's always true: if you want to see Jesus you have to look up to him.

Joining a group

I need 6 or 7 of you to help me.

One of the girls go and stand on the far left-hand side.

The rest of you make a huddle on the far right.

To the single girl: Now when I say 'GO' I want you to try to get into that huddle.

Ready? One, two, three: GO!

(Most times she will have to struggle and the huddle strive to keep her out . . . otherwise use the alternative below.)*

All right. STOP!

I told her to try to get in.
I did ***not*** tell you to try to keep her out!

That happens far too often.

In some countries or towns or clubs or schools all kinds of people are kept out and not allowed to join because they are the wrong colour or speak a different language or come from a different country.

There are even some churches where people go to join and feel they are not wanted.

Let's start again.

To the girl: All you have to do is say, 'Please may I come in?'

She does so and she is accepted.

And it is best of all if one of you from the group goes and brings her in.

One of the group goes and fetches her.

(* Not all countries, towns, communities are like that and they welcome other people who want to join them.)

Never let your group refuse anyone who wants to join

and most of all, don't ever let people feel they are not wanted in your church.

The best thing to do is to go and invite people to join and to *bring* them.

The right cheek

How many of you are right-handed?

(Select a volunteer.) Will you please come here?

Now, will you *very gently* hit me on the cheek?

Fine. That was my left cheek.

Now with your right hand will you *gently* hit me on the right cheek? *(Has to be back-handed.)*

You see – the only way for a right-handed person to hit someone on the right cheek is with the back of their hand.

And a back-handed slap is about the worst insult you could give to a Jewish person.

So, when one day Jesus said to his followers:

'If anyone strikes you on the right cheek offer him also the left.' (*Matthew 5:39)*

He was teaching them *and us*: 'Even if somebody insults you as badly as they can, you must keep on loving them.'

Read Matthew 5:38–42.

From here on the addresses are equally suitable for use in church and for school assemblies.

The farmer and his cows

(Ask a man – dressed for the part if possible – to take the part of the farmer.)

Good morning, Mr Farmer. It's a lovely day.

Farmer Aye, it is that. Good morning to ye.

That's a fine horse you have there.

Farmer Aye, she is that. Had her since she was a foal but she's the only one I've got now.

What would you do if you had two horses now?

Farmer Ah'd sell one – and gi'e the money to the poor.

Is that your tractor in the corner of the field?

Farmer Aye. Ah'd be lost wi'out it, couldn't get the harvest in.

Tell me, what would you do if you had two tractors?

Farmer Well, Ah suppose Ah'd sell one, and gi'e the money to the poor.

Do you live in that splendid farmhouse over there?

Farmer Aye. Lived there all me life.

I hardly dare to ask – but suppose you had two farmhouses. What would you do?

Farmer You can guess – Ah'd sell one and gi'e the money to the poor.

That's a great-looking cow in that field.

Farmer Aye, she is that.

I have to ask: what would you do if you had two cows?

Farmer Keep 'em!

Now just a minute. If you had two horses or tractors or farmhouses you'd sell one and give the money to the poor.

But you would keep the two cows. Why?

Farmer Ah've got two cows – in fact Ah've got twenty – and Ah'm not selling them.

It's so easy to dream about what you would like to do.

What matters is what you *actually* do.

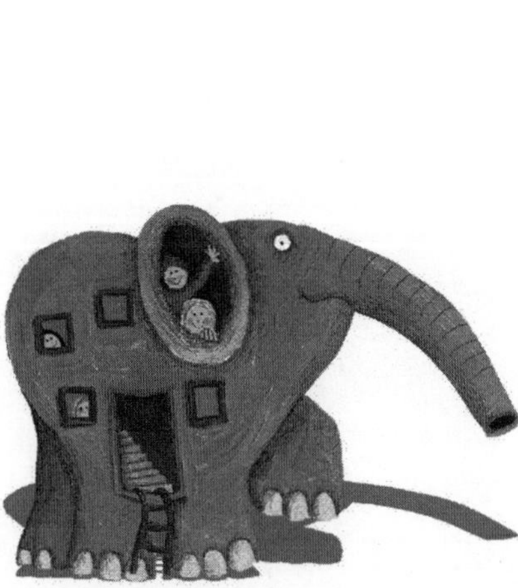

Eating dog food

(Beforehand, very carefully remove the top from a tin of Pal – or another well-known dog food. Empty and clean the tin and refill with milk-softened Weetabix. Carefully replace the lid so the tin looks unopened.)

Talk with children about having dogs as pets and tins of dog food. During this conversation clearly open the tin and move towards the children, offering them a spoonful.

When two or three have responded, 'No', 'No thanks' or 'No way', eat two or three spoonfuls yourself and explain:

It's not dogfood – it's Weetabix.
It might say Pal *(or xxx)* on the tin – but inside it's Weetabix.
What matters is what's inside.

Some people outwardly look very nice and kind
but what matters is what's inside.

What matters most is not your outward appearance
but what's in your heart.

Looking at a box

(Take a carton – 46cm x 30cm or so – with a large, very different picture on each side and put it in a large bin bag.)

(Set a group of children to your right and left.)

I've got a box with a picture on it.

Take it out of the bag and hold it in front of you.

To the left-hand group:

What's this a picture of? *(e.g. a horse)*

To the right-hand group:

What's this a picture of? *(e.g. a train)*

Now, just a minute. Didn't you say it was a horse? And *you* think it's a train? Can't you tell the difference between a horse and a train?

And when I ask the people in front of me, which do you think it is, a horse or a train? *(e.g. an apple)*

Now the penny drops.

You can all see it's a box with a picture on it
but you all see different pictures.

You on my left can see what the others can't see,
and you on my right can see what the others can't see,
and you in front of me can see what the others can't see
and I can see what none of you can!

If we want to know what others can see we have to ask them or listen to them.

Christians need to listen to Muslims and Muslims to Christians.

Arabs need to listen to Jews and Jews to Arabs.

Parents need to listen to children and children to parents.

Nobody can see everything or know everything.

We all need to listen to and learn from each other.

The elephant

This story has the same message as 'Looking at a box'.

(Get three boys blindfolded and a fourth as chamberlain to help you.)

King Peter had three courtiers who really got on his nerves.

They were supposed to advise him but they could never agree about anything.

Each of them was always sure that he was right and the others wrong.

So he devised a plan to teach them a lesson.

He sent the chamberlain to bring in the first. *(He does so.)*

King Peter said, 'Hello Alfie, my friend King Johannes has sent me a very special gift. Please hold it here and can you tell me what it is?'

He made the courtier stand and hold it.

'Oh, Your Majesty,' he said. 'What a wonderful gift! This is a bell rope and King Johannes has sent you a bell tower so whenever there is any danger we can ring the bell to warn you and all the people.'

'Stay there, Alfred,' said King Peter, 'and we'll send for Robert.'

He sent the chamberlain to bring in the second courtier.

(The chamberlain does so.)

'Hello, Bobby,' he said. 'Sorry about the blindfold but my friend King Johannes has sent me a very special gift and I wonder if you can play this game and tell me what it is?'

He led the blindfolded Robert to the gift and gave him part of it to hold.

'Oh, Your Majesty,' he said, 'What a surprising gift! We've already got one fire engine and this must be another! As I hold this hosepipe I must say we shall have no danger of burning at all.'

'I told you it was special,' said the King. 'Stand where you are and the chamberlain can go and get Charles.'

(The chamberlain does so.)

'Hello, Charlie,' the King said. 'Sorry about the blindfold but I wonder if you will play this game with us.

'My friend King Johannes has sent me a very special gift. Please kneel here, hold it and tell me what it is.'

Charles did as directed.

'Well, Your Majesty, it might be a fine, old tree with this gnarled trunk and I'm sure it's a very generous gift but surely we've got enough trees already with the finest forests of any country!'

'That's wonderful,' said King Peter. 'Alfred thinks it's a bell tower, Robert thinks it's a fire engine, and Charles thinks it's a tree.

'Well, you can't all be right. In fact, none of you is!

'Chamberlain, remove their blindfolds so they can see what they've really been holding.'

He did as commanded and the confused courtiers saw that

Alfred was holding a tail

Robert was holding a trunk

and Charles was holding a leg

and that in fact it was . . .

WHAT?

Yes! An elephant!

And King Peter said, 'I get tired of you three always arguing and thinking you alone know what's right. When will you ever learn that nobody can see everything or know everything. We all need to listen to and learn from each other.'

That's the message:

We all need to listen to and learn from each other.

Christians need to listen to Muslims and Muslims to Christians.

Arabs need to listen to Jews and Jews to Arabs.

Parents need to listen to children and children to parents.

Nobody can see everything or know everything.

We all need to listen to and learn from each other.

George and the spoons

(You need a long-handled spoon and fork.)

If you go to a friend's party what is your favourite food?

(The children mention some foods.)

I must tell you about George and his dream.

George was very fat. The word has to be 'obese'. He only had one meal a day – which lasted from getting up in the morning to going to bed at night!

Well, George had a dream. He dreamt he was going down a passage with a lot of other fat boys and girls, all pushing against each other.

They went through double swing-doors into a large hall and George had never seen so much food – there were lots of tables absolutely loaded with food *(mention examples you were given earlier)* and George's favourite – jelly and custard and trifle!

The man in charge said, 'You are very welcome to this party and you can eat as much food as you like.'

George could hardly believe his ears – nobody had ever said that to him before.

The man said, 'But there's a small snag – you can't touch any food with your hands!'

'I knew it,' thought George, 'all this lovely food and I'm not allowed to touch it.'

'But we shall give each of you a spoon and a fork, both with long handles,' said the man.

'Hey, that's good,' thought George, 'not as good as a handful but I shall need a spoon to get some trifle.'

'Oh, there's another small thing – the spoon and the fork will be fastened to your upper arm – at the elbow!'

So George got his fastened on – like this.

(Hold the fork to your left elbow and try to eat a cake which will not reach your mouth.)

He tried again with a vol-au-vent and again with a piece of pizza, with the same result.

'I'll do better with the spoon,' he thought.

(Hold the spoon to your right elbow and enact his efforts.)

So he tried again – with a spoonful of crisps – but he spilled them on the floor.

He tried again with some peanuts on his spoon – and flicked them into the air – and managed to catch only one in his mouth. So he tried again – and caught two!

Feeling a bit more hopeful as he chewed his three peanuts he thought he would try with trifle. He took one large spoonful and flicked it in the air – and it landed on his head!

So he went on again and again. He was getting in a terrible mess – with all his favourite food on the floor, his hair, and his face, with very little in his mouth.

Then he noticed two children doing quite well.

(Get a boy and a girl to the front to help you. Hold the fork on the arm of the boy, and then the spoon on the arm of the girl.)

The boy speared a piece of cake with his fork and held it for the girl to eat. *(They do so.)*

The girl got a spoonful of trifle and gave it to the boy.
(They do so.)

The message is very plain.
If you only look after yourself you'll get in an awful mess.
We are supposed to help other people.

Fingers arguing

(Use your left hand for the following address.)

One day the fingers had an argument.

The thumb folded his arms and said, 'I must be the best because I'm stronger than all of you put together!'

When you pick up your hymn book you can see what he meant. Thumbs on one side and all the fingers on the other.

Show thumb: This one stands for Strength.

This one stands for Strength.

'Just a minute,' said the forefinger,
'I think it's much more important to show people the way.'

If I asked you the way to the *(chemist)*,
you would say: down the street that way – pointing – and . . .
(give some directions).

Pointing out the right way is also giving an Example.

Show forefinger: This one stands for Example.

This one stands for Example,
this one for Strength, this one for Example.

(Interchange thumb and forefinger.)

Suddenly the middle finger joined in:
'What about Beauty?

I'm the tallest, so I must be better than you two!

If I was shorter, a hand would be all angular and jagged.'

(Show how.)

'I give the hand its shape, its unity, its beauty.'

So this one stands for Beauty.

This one for Strength, this one for Example, and this one for Beauty.

(Interchange fingers as you wish.)

Then another finger joined in the argument – the fourth.

What would you wear on this finger? *(A ring)*

So, what do you think this finger stands for?

Marriage/Love

Yes, it stands for Love.

So now there are four fingers arguing about who is the most important. *(Interchange fingers as you like.)*

Suddenly the little finger shouted,
'Stop! Will you all stop arguing? Please!

Look, I'm not very strong
and no one uses me to point out the way
unless they are very posh! *(mimicking)*
And I'm not very tall
and I'm not the Love finger.

But if you put your hands together to say your prayers
I'm furthest from you and nearest to other people.
I have to remind you about Unselfishness.'

Unselfishness is your real Strength, the best Example,
the true Beauty and essential for Love.

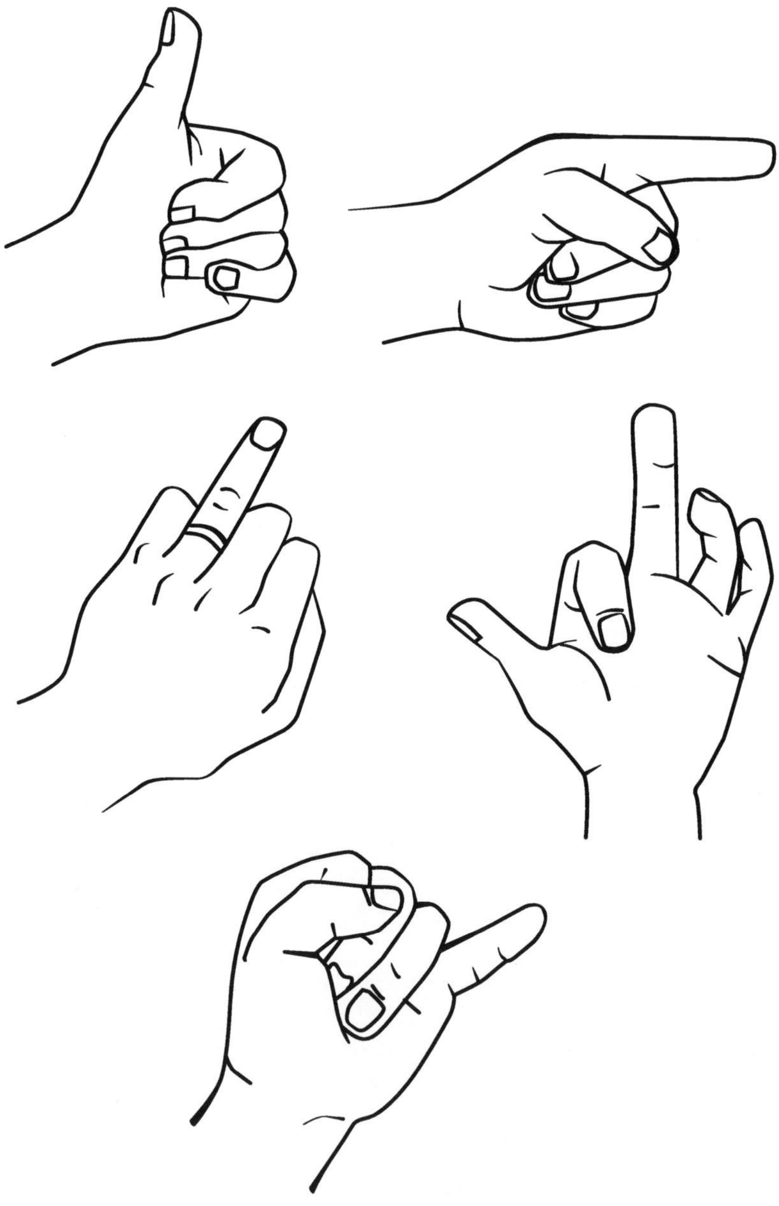

Harvest Scrabble

(You need a large rack – as in Scrabble *– and the 7 letters.)*

What words can you make from these letters?

S H E V A R T

(Arrange the letters as the following words are suggested and announce their scores.)

HAVE – 10
HATE – 7
RAVE – 7
RATE – 4
VEST – 7
HEAR – 7
TEAR – 4
HEART – 8
SHAVE – 11

and conclude by recalling and high-lighting

HARVEST	**STARVE**	**SHARE**	**EARTH**
13	9	8	8

HARVEST reminds us that because millions STARVE

we have to SHARE

and we have to SHARE the EARTH.

Sharing an apple

(Give a small apple to one of the children – ask them to eat it now and save you the core.)

We have been given an apple to share.

(Cut a very small slither from one side.)

Is this fair? *(No)*

(Cut a larger slither from one side.)

Is it fair now? *(No)*

(Cut another slice but still not half.)

Well, is it fair now? *(No)*

I'll tell you how to do it:

If two of you are given an apple to share,
you say to your friend,

'You cut – I'll choose!'

Their tongue comes out, and they cut very carefully before you choose to make sure you only get half!

We are not very good at sharing.

Can I have that core back please?

At harvest time we are reminded that half the world is hungry but we are not very good at sharing.

We are given the earth to share but we are not very good at sharing.

Too often we give to hungry people the scraps we don't want.

(Throw the apple core carelessly aside.)

Or we hope they will be satisfied if we let them have a mere slither, like when we cut the apple.

We are given the earth to share.

The Third World

Hands up if you have heard of the Third World.

Can you tell me where it is?

And where is the First World?

And the Second World?

I have only just learned the truth about it.

I used to think the First World is Europe
and the Second World is America
which was called the New World
and the Third World is the rest.

I was quite wrong.

The phrase was first used by Mr Nehru, the first Prime Minister of an independent India, when America and Russia were fiercely opposed to each other in what was called the Cold War – no fighting but lots of threats and threatening behaviour.

It turns out that by the First World he meant America, Europe and Australia, by the Second World he meant Russia and its allies and the Third World meant Africa, India, and South America.

Since then we have learned that the poorest people live in what Mr Nehru called the Third World.

First or last, Second or Third, old or new,

as you know very well there is only one world

and we are meant to live in peace

and share it

until none is hungry.

Tea or coffee

Often at the end of a service (assembly) I am glad to have a cup of coffee or a cup of tea, with milk and one sugar.

I've got some questions about where all the constituents of a cup of coffee or a cup of tea come from.

And I don't want you to say Tesco's or Morrisons, Asda or Sainsbury's, or any supermarket or shop!

Where does coffee come from? *(Brazil)*

Where does tea come from? *(India)*

Where does sugar come from? *(West Indies)*

Where does milk come from? *(Milkman/cows)*

Where does water come from? *(The tap)*

Brazil, India, the West Indies, England – so many countries

and so many people

growing, picking, packing, loading, shipping, unloading, transporting, unloading, manufacturing, driving, stacking shelves . . .

All so I can have a cup of coffee or a cup of tea.

When you get home try making a list of how many people are involved so *you* can have a drink.

We take too much for granted.